CW00471738

festo

in festo nativitatis

Alwyn Marriage

Oversteps Books

First published in 2012 by   Oversteps Books Ltd
6 Halwell House
South Pool
Nr Kingsbridge
Devon
TQ7 2RX
UK

www.overstepsbooks.com

Copyright © 2012 Alwyn Marriage
ISBN 978-1-906856-32-8

All rights reserved. No part of this book may be reproduced,
stored in a retrieval system, or transmitted in any form, or by
any means, electronic, mechanical, photocopying, recording
or otherwise, or translated into any language, without prior
written permission from Oversteps Books, except by
a reviewer who may quote brief passages in a review.

The right of Alwyn Marriage to be identified as the author of
this work has been asserted by her in accordance with the
Copyright, Designs and Patents Act 1988.

Printed in Great Britain by imprint digital, Devon.

Zoë, Sophia and Hugh

Acknowledgements:

A number of these poems have been published in the followii
magazines, anthologies and collections:
*Beautiful Man (Outposts 1977), New Christian Poetry
(Collins 1990), Challenges Anthology (Biscuit Publishing
2005), Touching Earth (Oversteps 2007), Orta Christmas
Anthology (Poetry on the Lake 2009), Poetry in the Waiting
Room 2012 and Christian Journal.*

Extracts from *'Epiphany'* were broadcast on the *BBC World
Service.*

I am grateful to the team at Little Gidding who invited me to
present a programme of my Christmas poetry there, and
encouraged me to put together this collection for others to use
as a resource.

Thanks, also, to Canon Jeremy Davies who in two consecutive
Advents preached sermons at Salisbury Cathedral on poems
included in this collection.

Contents

Author's note

For years our family has sent out one of my poems as a
Christmas card, and several of the poems in this collection
were written in response to that annual expectation. Many of
them have been used at Christmas events by those who have
received or shared them, and they are now being made
available for more general use. Christmas comes round so
quickly each year, and there is always a need for new material
for concerts, services and other events. I hope some of these
poems may make a useful contribution to the festivities.

Double concept

Who could possibly conceive
of such a preposterous
idea?

Even the breath of wind
that pushed a door ajar,
hesitated for a timeless moment

as a young girl gasped
in horror that she should have thought it,
sickened at the faintest stirring
in her womb, or deep in the recesses
of her mind.

No birdsong could be heard
not even the cooing of a dove
as fear and questioning began to form
within.

Why was she chosen
to conceive of such a possibility;
to harbour the germ of an idea
that ached with infinite potential
and turned the whole of human history
on its axis?

Annunciation

after Simone Martini

Not one short moment in eternity,
fleeting of fear in the dove's flight,
but the opening of a door you have peeped through before
then crept back, avoiding infinity.
You cannot refuse, though already
your body aches with the world's redeeming pain.
Mary, pawn of God, be now his queen.

Stone circle

The days are lengthening,
shadows of the stones at midday
shrinking to a pool.

Enigmatic and immovable, a well
of theories and wild suppositions
taunts our search for certainty:

moon time, sun time, sacrifice,
almanac for planting, feast and frenzied
orgy at each solstice celebration.

Through the ages hands have stroked
the surface of these megaliths, and fingers poked
into every dark inviting crevice;

but still the stones
turn their backs on idle gaze
to hide their meaning.

Even on the shortest night
mystery dances in the moonlight;
no hint, not even remnants of a rune

to indicate whether our prehistoric ancestors
celebrated late December or high June
as the pivot of the ever-turning year.

Michaelmas

St Michael summons frolicking angels
from their play and recreation.

All summer long they soaked up sunshine,
stored their energy for darker days.

Today, in a flutter of wings, angelic lights
begin to burn defiantly as earth turns dark side up,

the flame set on economy, conserving
power, since light must last all winter.

After the shortest day they'll blaze
with brief but potent memories of sheep fields,

before the long months when the light will seem to fade,
flickering to nothing one Friday late in Spring.

Uncertain Advent
December 2002

Can Christmas this year pierce the gathering darkness,
the daily news that plays upon our fear?
Apocalyptic premonitions shape our Advent,
that even in the throb of Christmas preparation
war and the plots of terrorists are ever near.
Christmas may warm our hearts,
but not till wintry chill
has seeped through sinew, heart and bone
with threat of horrors yet unknown.

Stars and angels tell a different story,
of unquenched light and peace and warm goodwill;
a message scattering stardust down the ages
encouraging us to trust that all may yet be well.
Through darkest night a glimmer leads to morning,
guiding our hope and trust and longing still.

Waiting in the dark we cannot know
what lies ahead, of war or of redemption.
What images assail us in the night,
of rape and pillage, show
of rage and might; or light
of long lost sweet remembered love?
Through the dark hours our thoughts are turned and tossed;
we snatch at tantalising dreams of reconciliation
gently ruffling feathers on the white breast
of a dove.

Before the morning comes
we wait, as night
aches on. Uncertain now
what shape or form
our longing calls to birth;
knowing only that those who take up arms
will never bless this earth.

Yet even now we dare to trust our longing,
that when the first faint glow
of morning washes darkness from our eyes,
all that our hearts were yearning for in darkness,
will like a radiant, Christmas morning,
rise.

Solstice

trees gaze down silently
at shivering reflections
as chill water circles roots

midwinter heaves its Janus head
to face both ways and
counts the days

dusk fades, the shortest day
is sleeping, seeping into longest night
transfixed on the axis of the year

nature's see-saw hits the bottom
with a bump   a glimpse
of light leaks weakly through the darkness

frozen briefly into midnight stillness
the year is turning, turning: memory
fading into future hope

Hope at year's turning

The twelfth stroke makes its statement firm and clear.
As midnight closes I, too, draw a line
and through the darkness turn to face the day
more new, unspoilt and full of promises
than those I've chewed at, choked on
and spat out,
that now lie well behind me.

After such a year, what can we hope for?
What stake our lives on? Is there still a spark
that flickers through the darkness we have known?

Neither wishful thinking nor assurance;
poised between faith, coin of the Church,
and love, 'the best of all',
hope springs eternal,
leaps and bounds,
believes in bud, and leaf and flower,
and puppy-like joyfully welcomes friend and foe.
Against all recent evidence I throw
myself into the arms of hope
for the new year.

Re-painting Mary's gown

It was painted in blue
of a summer's day,
or the shade that hides in the glacial ice
of cold virginity.

Try white for the purity
of an innocent girl,
of the unspotted bed linen
in a romantic tale;

or red for the guilt
of a bastard bump,
for illicit passion
and a crucified tramp

Never in black,
despite sorrow and sword
and a pondering heart
that accepted God's word.

Paint it in green
for the promise of growth,
for words that bear fruit
in a harvest of truth.

Festive

It's common to complain about the panic of preparation,
the struggle to perform essential tasks like shopping,
the endless round of cooking, washing up
and making small talk, and the cost of purchasing
the smallest token of our love for family and friends.

But in the swirl and whirl of festive food
and excess alcohol there sometimes dawns
a kernel of understanding, just the germ of an idea
that maybe there is something here
worth celebrating.

The feast inspires some tiny miracles that we might miss:
when else do we sit down and think about
our friends, however briefly,
write a message to them or, at least,
sign our name and send a two-stroke kiss?

On Christmas Eve when shops at last are shut,
the lights and decorations that we dig out every year
are draped around the tree, we've stacked the 'fridge
with food, arranged the crackers on the tables
and stored away the paper, sellotape and labels;

then our thoughts can turn again to stories told
down more than twenty centuries, and as we hear
the well-known carols, the truth that's packed
inside this festival might re-emerge,
turning our simplest acts of giving to pure gold.

Then our love comes packaged
Father Christmas style:
a satsuma, an apple
and a handful of mixed nuts
snuggling deep into the toe
of half a pair of tights.

Three short moments in eternity

After the pain, the rush of blood,
there was a healing hush in the peace
of animals with steaming breath. Then came
the tramp of feet, a stream of visitors
bearing compliments and gifts,
and words that soon began to sound
like infant theology.

Shh: just for an hour
let me be,
to wonder at this mystery of life,
to play.

Ecce homo. Listen. Watch,
as hungry for a miracle
the masses try to touch
the man for others.
Jostling curiosity
turns to raucous hate
as rabble raisers hiss and cry
three cheers, then Crucify!

Wait:
is there time
to sit and listen at his feet,
and while others rush about in haste,
to dream?

Clamour of tongues
clattering down the ages;
chatter of churches,
doctrine in heady doses,
clash of religious wars;
hierarchy and privilege,
restrictive, life-denying laws.

Drawn by love,
I slip
into the silence of eternity,
gaze
on God.

Logos

God said
    'I give you my Word'.

Before the music of the spheres,
    a word;
before the Milky Way was drawn
across the darkness of
    the heavenly void,
or solar storms and sunsets
mixed chaotic colours, splashed
across earth's darkest skies,
or charmed its muted moods
to glow with vibrant light:
    a word.

Stars spun, theological dust storms
swirled down the centuries,
chattering and raging.
Maybe its meaning
could have been clearer;
the occasional hint
given to explain why
God was revealed in a baby's cry.

Worlds have turned, planets exploded,
constellations collapsed; clatter and chatter
have crowded out the silence
in which that word
was spoken.

But still it is heard
sometimes
in song, or poem
or love letter;

and still the promise finds expression
in the laughter of small children
and the patience of the gardener,
in the passion of the lover
and the antics of the clown.

Cold Comfort

Yes baby, well may you cry
the trouble you've caused.
Love of drama on somebody's part is responsible
for the tragedy and pathos, contradiction and paradox.
A father who isn't your father
A mother without a husband
soon to lose her son, but not so soon
as others who knew nothing of your birth
who went obediently forth and multiplied,
only to lose their own because you have been born.
You, christened 'God with us'
mighty God of all power
supposedly anthropomorphised by a feeble, dirty
son of much-maligned-by-gossip mother,
not even refugeed, just come too late
to where, but for others, there would have been room.
You, nick-named Love, born without the love-act
of parents, who, it seems, had not embraced
full physical joys of consummated love.

You're not the first to feel the pangs
of being born.
Others have more to cry about
but weaker lungs to make their misery known.
No bombs threaten you, no starvation
wrinkles your mother's breast and makes her nipple
pale, useless, uncomforting, a dehydrated pea.
Straw's quite warm, compared with nothing,
whatever swaddling bands may be
or how friendly the animals feel
to the wailing intruder.
The stable, an unfortunate necessity for a day or two,
later to be cherished as romantic dreams of youth
by a comfortable mother in a Nazareth home.
However abnormal your family, they care for each other,
giving you security and human love.
You feel no crippling pains, nor even have
a shameful handicap to cry about.
For thirty years, all that a man may want is yours.

Why is it, then, that in your cry I hear
the misery of the world?
and in your eyes I see
comprehension and forgiveness of everything,
including me?
Why is it in your birth it seems
everyone is born?
and in your utter helplessness
God's strength is shown?

Unhappy baby, do not cry for me.
Maturity will bring the need to die for me
so save your tears.
Choke your breath in the straw
to escape the death of living
knowing all.
Harden your heart, to avoid the open wounds of feeling
all, for all.
Leave it to another to be God's son,
Go back and suggest to Him it's too much for one
man to bear. Beg Him to share
the burden between all babies
past, present and to come.

Then return, and just cry for your milk.

Song of the sentimental cow, the cynical sheep and the stubborn donkey

i
When I drop a calf
I bellow loud and long,
spreading the message far and near
that new life has begun.

This human heifer groaned to bring
a world to birth; offered
no rasping tongue to clean the child,
but wrapped him up in strips of cloth
and held him close.
My udder quivered with delight
to see him drink so deep
of human milk.

I couldn't sleep that night:
strange sounds were drifting from the hills
to echo in my ears and make me think
that I could hear the music of the spheres;
and pregnant stars, trembling with light
grew clearer still, until the sky
was bright as day.

Mm, moo, mooo,
moooonlight outshone by starlight.

ii
What sort of birthday present is this?

My former masters shuffled in
with steamy breath and muddy boots,
bringing their gift, a lamb

torn from the teat
and comforting warm wool
to be the shepherds' sacrificial gift,
to satisfy their whim.

They clearly didn't stop to think
who'd feed this little one,
or what sort of human child would want
this offering:

a feeble lamb, untimely born,
now motherless.
Baa, baa
barmy idea if you ask me.

iii
Eyes firmly shut, I twitch
one ear and hear a human infant's cry.
I will not look for fear
they'll make me rise and bear
another load. My knees still ache
from the long journey, will not bend, because
although my contract was to carry a mere girl,
and being a gentle, well-bred donkey I should not complain,
she bore a child, who seemed to carry with him
the world's great weight of pain.

Although my master has a gentle touch,
eeyor, eeyor
'e always makes me carry far too much.

Have a drink on me

I missed the fancy bit:
you know, the alleluyas, heavenly choirs,
all that, though come to think
of it, I swear I did see stars
as I was lumbering up the hill;
and the girl at the village watering hole
is something of an angel.

Anyway, when I got back,
a little worse for wear
and expecting all the other blokes
to have a go at me for being late,
they were all of a giggle and scuffle
as happy as a cart-load of drunks
though they swore they were plain cold sober.

They were just leaving,
yes, I mean leaving the sheep
there on the hillside, and could hardly
get their story straight. Well,
if there was something interesting about to happen,
I was up for it. So off I went with the rest.

When we all trooped into a stable,
I reckoned perhaps I'd gone too far
with the drink this time;
I mean, for heaven's sake,
what were we doing there?

They did their homage bit, I smiled
and nodded, didn't let them down;
then as my head was throbbing fit to burst
I settled myself in a corner on the straw
and promptly fell asleep.
I hope I didn't snore.

When I woke up, everything seemed clearer,
brighter. The kids with their love-child
seemed pleased that I was rested, even let
me hold the baby.

I clutched him like a new-born lamb.
He looked up at my face
as though he knew me, chuckled
when he smelled my breath,
clutched at my grubby finger.

I breathed his sweetness in,
great gulps of milky baby flesh
and innocence. It filled my lungs
and kept me smiling when I left the shed.

I still haven't got a clue what it was all about;
but have a feeling celebration is in order.
All of a sudden, life doesn't seem as bad
as I thought it was. Come on:
have a drink on me.

Cheers.

Soft as a feather falling

Why should a stork glide over a golden palace,
pause, drop a feather, then fly on?

Encircling the splendour of a temple,
wings slowly flap, then beat a little faster
as a feather flutters down.

High over the financial centre of the city
she hesitates, takes a deeper breath,
closes her eyes to avoid the sight
of avarice, then plunges past,
sharing, with perceptive pity,
the lightest touch of white.

She flies on over arid stony ground
where greedy men are fighting over land,
hears keening, whistling, feels a searing pain
sees a drop of red form on her breast
and in return offers up the lightness
of her own pure whiteness.

Out in the hills again, she catches
first rays of a new dawn,
hears the faintest snatches of unearthly music,
circles high over an unlit village
where she watches as a feather catches moonlight
as it spirals to the ground.

Her journey almost over,
the stork flies low
sits on a humble roof
apparently quite unconcerned
by all the drama
down below.

She shakes herself, feeling the chill winds
around her body as more feathers fall
to form a cosy nest and bring some comfort
to a fledgeling's bed:
white, with a speck of red.

Epiphany: A journey

I

Who were they, the men poised between reality and myth?
Kings? Wise men? Strangers from a far away land?
Did they breathe stardust, leave it lying around
for us to breathe again? Were they aware
of their existence; question the notion
of a transcendent deity? If they perceived,
through the unfortunate coincidence of being wise,
the magnitude of their revelation, did they immediately
slip from the confines of the temporal
into the liberty of infinity?

O Come, Come,
Come King Emmanuel,
Don't want this Jesus-baby
Wrapped up in tinsel;
but the crystallized moments
of heaven on earth,
the stillness, the crying,
the silent shriek
of Adam's consummation.

II

The journey was longer than I ever dreamt it could be
and taught me many new variants of pain:
the aching body which had served me well
only to be punished by longer, harder miles;
the stones which looked innocuous on the road
but through my sensible boots still pierced my feet
like stars; the panic when I wandered
onto a field of stubble-burning.

Listen to the murmuring of living reeds around the stagnant pool,
the dry grass crackling among the tombs by the deserted church.
Remember the failed friendship, the one who was frightened by love,
dared not hope, feared to test his faith which sadly flew away
leaving only feathers.
The chickens are scattered, weep over Jerusalem,
Jerusalem so loved, but not the end of the journey.
Because I hope to walk without cheating
I must walk into hell to die.

III

Mephistopheles depressive, I will not come with you,
though you use the voice of reason, for
I've been your way before.

nor will I fear this lonely land again
which I must pass through with unblinkered eyes
wishing for blindness and release.

Although the pain will be as deep in rediscovery
it's possible that someone's waiting on the other side
to guide my way.

no answers will be given or comfort found,
the aching void will not be filled or dimmed
but I must enter without sinking.

when new eyes opening see light and
shade as one, lilac will fade
as rose comes into bloom.

Weave away!
the weft is new and strong, the thread like gold.
Infinite patterns dazzle my eyes
but will the warp hold?

IV

Fecisti nos ad te et inquietum est cor nostrum
donec requiescat in te *. Fecisti nos ad te, but still
we do not know where they were coming from;
et inquietum est cor nostrum, screaming in the night,
within our consistent systems which hit others at a tangent
only to be repelled when they lack light.
Donec, the cadence unresolved and aching,
donec, newspaper headline like a stained glass window
sings 'Beware the death of ideals: Helder Camara
relights the flames', but how can we
sing a new song in a foreign land?

Beware also the satisfying of needs, for your need may have built
the satisfaction; *requiescat*, brother from another womb
whose mother knows me not, I am carrying your sin and weakness
on this journey, find it heavy, stumble, rise and stumble with
            the weight.
But still I love you, still would offer
almost anything upon the shrine of our lost friendship,
but now am less sure what this love might mean.
Tutto mi porta a te. You are older
have been walking longer through the night;
was I unreasonable to suppose that you'd be further
on the road than I was, towards the light?
requiescat in te, when cessation of walking
will not be regretted when putting in motion again,
since movement has ceased at the journey's end
where position and momentum of every particle unite.

* *'Thou has made us for thyself and our hearts are restless till they find*
their rest in thee.' St Augustine, Confessions I, ch. 1

V

Into the stillness help me to go,
not the stillness of sunflower heliotrope
or of seagull taut-winged borne along wind
or of bodies close resting when passion is spent
but the stillness of midnight dark.

Into the darkness lead me:
not darkness of lights extinguished awaiting rekindling
or breathless submersion when water is over my head
or where faith illuminates and so negates,
but darkness where I must be alone.

Into aloneness I wander,
not holding the hand of lover or child
or friend sharing and breathing in time;
no one can descend with me or wait on the other side,
alone I must reach the depths of weakness.

To weakness may I submit;
small insect on the path awaits the crushing boot
whose inevitable falling is not cruel or kind;
rejecting those who fear my suffering and encourage me to cheat
I learn that only in weakness may perfect stillness be embraced.

VI

¡Oh dichosa ventura! [*1] Men or metaphors
travelling westward, obedient to a silent call;
much was left behind, and I imagine
there were friends who should have joined you on the road
who feared the dangers or could not believe
that anything would come of such a journey.

At least you were protected by covering new ground,
found nothing to remind you of those you left behind;
but did you ever groan as a wave of pain
was born over desert sands by a cruel night wind,
find yourselves whispering a name?
Averte oculos tuos a me,
quia ipsi me avolare fecerunt. [*2]

Singing to stop their tears, wisdom's march is slow;
laughing with the receding stars, unsure which way to go.
Where is he who is born, for we have seen his star?
Oh child, is that your star that shines so bright?
Will it be worth it, will they regret when they discover
the journey's end is different from the source of light?

[*1] *St John of the Cross, Songs of the soul in rapture: 'Oh venture of delight!'*
[*2] *Song of Songs, chapter 6 verse 5. 'Turn away your eyes from me, for they
have overwhelmed me.'*

VII

Like Eudoxus I'd be prepared to embrace
the fate of Phaethon, if by that sacrifice
I'd learn the sun's nature, magnitude and form.

Where there is no vision the people perish
and every way we turn we see them wither
because they close their eyes.

Tregeagle stoops again to lift waters of life,
hears laughter, turns to catch a fleeting glimpse
of Athene-fly-by-night.

Regret is inappropriate response to the inevitable,
and wisdom the foolishness of giving up all to travel
where those most educated claim we cannot go.

My loves and hopes and all that I have stood for burn,
the will to live has vanished, but proscribed
is easy exit with a mortal death.

Finally I angrily throw beliefs into the fire,
then find faith, naked and trembling stands
rather self-consciously, but strong, with empty hands.

VIII

Sensing another song on the other side of silence,
words to be learnt that are far beyond learning,
music which moves in stillness, cannot be heard,
bringing peace only to the tormented.
I cannot be said to have learnt what is beyond learning,
have rather come to know, through my unknowing,
greatest peace is dearly bought with greatest suffering.

I only dared to give myself in truth to you
when I no longer feared to lose you, found
myself ready, if necessary, for the sacrifice.

Exploring the stillness of the holy Lotus
I swim across the river of pain
to breathe poised on the other side.

IX

But still we do not know
where they were coming from
or where they went when they
returned by another way
(show me the way).
We only know that they brought gifts,
symbols of our own life and experience.
I do not think such perfect symbols
had extension, took up space within
the real stable, or when God accepted them
there was a change in the visual field
of Jesus.

No gift can be brought to the world's source:
at best we can seek through metaphor
for the offering-up of intense experience
before the ultimate.
The slow and steady steps approach no throne;
the culmination of the world's deep wisdom
bows before the unknown.

X

We do not know where they were coming from,
but we must learn to lose and still to love,
to love yet willingly let go.

Myrrh-man murmuring
of sin to the innocent
sadness to the singers, doom
as from the womb spring
king and baby.

We do not know their route, what country they passed through,
yet find that faith holds us despite ourselves,
when all else is rejected, will not go.

Mystical moment in
movement of frankincense,
seared in the fire, till frank, intense
white heat of purity
kindled of Incarnation.

We cannot guess what lay ahead of them when they had seen
        the light:
we weep despairingly when the hope we live by seems deception,
but still accept its guidance for our life.

Gold, from one too old
to covet, to one too young to care.
Cold is the glow of gold
Child, beside your fire.

XI

Foolish trust, sweet innocence: the moon where your heart
   once cried;
was it because you could not fear enough you died?
Fools only know no fear: in that deep river
you gasped incarnate, and yet did not drown.

You learnt to swim in amnion before immersion
as neonate into the sea of death.
The star that I've been following is strangely reminiscent
of a cross, but kings in adulthood should wear a crown.

"I came
   to cast fire
     on the earth
      and would
       that it were
        already
KINDLED."

Holy holy holy
feathery green tamarisk ripening into mauve
(for if they do these things in a green tree
what shall be done in the dry?)

XII

Cry shame of the world on an unmarried mother,
for the darkness comprehended it not.
In an unspectacular village, where was no possession or belonging
he came unto his own and his own received him not.
We left our prejudices at a stable door
gave up the search for meaning in the mystery.

Mary
Mother of God
poor frightened girl
don't cry:
the child who brings
this shame on you
is Son
of the most High.

The earth's stomach turned over and God was born.
Beside this child our star shines not so bright,
a golden ear of corn given to Triptolemus
for spreading cultivation to humankind.
Our guiding light shrinks to a point within the heart,
a point is that of which there is no part.

Small creature of paradox,
God so small
forgive my disbelief;
the space that separates
this baby from the star
is smaller than it looks
but combusts with holocaustic fire.

We kneel with empty hands where the baby does not lie,
offer gifts more precious than those which can be possessed,
look for no acceptance, resume the road without a sigh,
taking fruits of the Spirit, now strangely reassessed.
Faith of Job, love of Jesus, hope of Jeremiah,
the way through death to holiness cannot avoid the fire.

XIII

Have I got the message right?
Ambiguous cross in the skies, are you presaging
a love that goes beyond reason, against reason,
isn't deserved, and quite honestly isn't desired?

I no longer need you on this journey, since the source of light
is nearer, though I weep that you were left on the other shore.
Having walked all night the dawn is brighter,
shows a new dimension opening bare but clear above.
The star remains to give direction through the darkness,
the light that emanates can never be reabsorbed,
is sharp, pure, sometimes agony, and bears the name of love.

XIV

Hope sings sweetest on the far side of despair,
confident that even that now lies within her embrace.
The caterpillar doesn't love the music
wrung by shafts of sunlight plucking pastel flowers,
has no faith in resurrection, but spins a cocoon for death,
then gently enters sleep, hoping for Anathoth.
Already Herod's infanticide is ringing in our ears,
the martyrdom of Stephen, loss of ideals, growth of fears.
Turning for home from the clear mountain top
we realise the road ahead of us is just as long
as the weary miles we have already come.

XV

And what of faith? Dear pilgrims
travelling, travelling painfully through the years,
not knowing where you're going to, forgetting
all the good and comfort that you've left behind.
You are wise, not arrogant, and therefore
carry no beliefs upon your shoulders;
progress is forward into unknowing, not resting
on static ritual, in which beauty still delights.
As each new tentative step is taken, becoming known,
so in becoming known is left behind, eyes
always piercing the darkness ahead of you,
the glow within you drawn forever on
towards the source of light.

Magi

They probably found it embarrassing
talking to an unknown baby,
rather like trying to utter words
in the ear of the dead beloved,
who always used to listen,
and respond.

Panel of the Isenheim altarpiece

Feathered Lucifer
a party pooper
at his Lord's nativity

despite his calm face
found he didn't quite know
how he should behave

and though he wouldn't
miss this Christmas party,
not for all the world,

while the baby radiated light
Lucifer, feathered like a holy dove,
looked the other way.

Weather warning

The woman on the radio
didn't mention the fact
that the sky would turn white, the air
between me and rest of the world
be obliterated in a whirl
of countless flakes, each one made up
of crystals of infinite, unique
complexity.

I don't remember her suggesting
we should watch out for the arrival
of this huge white conglomerate blob
of fluffy, weightless mass,
wandering coyly in my direction, then,
just as I put out my hand to capture its mystery,
veering off into wider space.

Did I hear her describe
the tickle on my nose when white
caressed it? Or the sparkling rainbow-gatherers
that clustered on my lashes?
Did she warn us that children from one to ninety
would shriek with excitement, jump as high
as nature allowed them, find themselves dancing
in time with the flurrying flakes;
or sit by the window, chin resting on hand,
time frozen as they gazed in wonder
at a world's instant transformation?

Did she predict
the sound of sledges sliding down iced
Christmas cakes; the hiss
of polished runners, cries
of exhilaration and alarm?

Did her report conclude with promises
of treats in store, wrapped in a sweet-sour
tingle as frozen flesh
thawed when we tumbled home?

I didn't hear her breathe a word
about the silent magic spreading down the country
from the north and blanketing in beauty
all the tawdry grime of yesterday;
or that ninety percent of a world-weary population
would greet this change in the weather
with joy and excitement. All
she offered us, in a voice drained of emotion,
was 'wintry precipitation'.

Constellation

Orion of the phallic belt and low slung sword
strides confidently every night across the winter's sky,
but shelters more coyly a nebula between his legs:
birthplace and nursery of our Milky Way.

Snowflake

In vague hesitation she touches my window
one satin slipper poised in delight
just for a moment
as the seven dwarfs wind whisks her snow white laughing sisters
on into the bottle green sea of tonight.

Unsure of her next move.
Should she join in the flick-flicking
flurrying dance
being swept to who-knows-where
from she-only-knows?
Or enter the spotlight, drunk with reflected glory
to pirouette and curtsey in the last dance of Icarus
on the warm winter glass
of my window?

– Brief indecision
brings a sadness.
Wait!
I only wanted to look through tear-stained eyelashes
into the light.

Too late.
She who once knew beauty, held
the world in her filigree web
now weeps into non-existence.

Ski scene

Controlling fear, contracting muscles, I wind
down curving piste while trying not to see
the plummeting depth below. I have to find
both strength and courage, so that I can ski.

As I reach the bottom a young girl joins the queue
before me for the lift. Unfit and overweight, she's
childishly dependent, out of place. I view
her mother help her hold the bar and point her skis.

Dragged back up to the dizzying height, I see
the girl stand close behind her mother, free her hand
then fearlessly follow her down the slope ahead of me.
My eyes are suddenly opened, and I understand:

Trusting the mother and skiing fast behind
requires great courage, for the child is blind.

January birthday

One feature of a Saturday birth in winter
is that football matches are more likely to occur,
some of which could prove to be
exceptionally memorable for one reason or another.

The day when I was born went down in family history
as the day that Arsenal beat Sunderland at home
4:1, and my father missed the match because
my mother was in labour.

As I was born at 6 o'clock in the evening
I've been enjoying the celebration of my birthday
all through the day today, without, so far,
the disadvantage of getting a year older.

Looking in the mirror I can't help wondering
what I'll look like thirty years from now –
assuming, that is, that I make it that far – and whether
by then I might have developed an interest in football.

Weight-bearing

Tree,
can you bear the weight
of all this gold and tinsel,
lights and star?

Can your frail branches hold
the winter's snow
that bows them to the ground,
bewitched in icing?

Can you resist
the buffeting of winds that whip
the woods into a frenzy of
exhileration and despair?

Tree, are you strong enough to carry
a bleeding, dying man
born crossways
on your bones?

And when you shivered in the Autumn
at the loss of all your leaves in scarlet pain,
did you trust that these vestigial buds would ripen
in the Spring again?

tree x

a tree
festive with pendulous globes
enclosing emptiness

green to set the teeth on edge
but clutching seeds of generation
germinating promise,

red ones, full of
bursting, juicing, spit-inducing
sweetness

high up, one golden sphere,
the key that might unlock a truth
elucidating some primaeval word

and, beguiling the lower branches,
a long thin shiny sinuous strand
of tempting tinsel

Pining

Conifers,
spruced up or noble, grace
homes, shops and parties,
decked as toys of tame festivity

but pining in defiant green
at the prospect of a dying year
and their wrenching exile
from the forest

where brown and golden ground is carpeted
with tears that fell
all down the rounding years,
soft, silent, still;

a wintry sun catches and glistens on
frosty fingers at the ends of branches,
staining the filigree shadows
playing down below;

darkness thickens,
a shimmering strand of long-dried grass
caught in a mesh of needles flutters,
before it's swallowed up in night.

By lying on the stone cold earth,
twisting round and squinting up, it's possible
to see a star, poised clear and sharp
above the apex of the tree.

The path through the woods

In summer this path's a dry and rutted
canvas on which ladybirds and beetles
scrawl their signatures.

But on this January afternoon I scrunch
a carpet of multi-coloured leaves, their shapes
merging into homogeneous decay.

Tentatively I pick my way around
the slippery sides of swamps and puddles,
balance as the mud betrays my feet.

The ground is specked with casual, natural
decoration: a magpie's wing, a small
white feather pressed down and preserved,

a tractor's steady pattern bearing in a rut
the shocking lime green of a piece
of fallen lichen;

and somewhere, far below,
hidden from the damp and frost,
a dream of Spring is forming.

In praise of white

A month ago snow
dropped overnight and lay
for several days,
obliterating mud and all the debris
of a wind-torn autumn.

Now snowdrops spread their tenderness
over the just recovering earth,
hinting at Spring with subtle scent
and slightest stature, unaware
that their modest purity is waking
a sun-starved world to a new year
and gracing gardens, lanes and woods
with unexpected, breath-arresting
beauty.

How strange to find
as colour starts to thread
the edges of the hedgerows
that the prettiest purple violets
lack the sweet seductive perfume
casually exhaled by their
diminutive white sisters.

March erupts in exuberant froth
of blossom as blackthorn covers
all its sharpest, darkest thorns
with the innocence
of white.

Wait until
April lights the shadows
underneath the trees,
when wood anemones will play
a similar tune. I find myself
smiling at the memory
of foreign friends who thought
that I was taking them to see
some wooden enemies,
only to find themselves
caught up in silent wonder
at the sheer fragility
of these pale wind flowers.

Colours move on through the months,
from yellow of late April, blue
of May to all the romance of pink June;
but still the memory will linger
that the first excitement of the year
was white.

Bud-break

Some buds open slowly out of winter,
stretch cautiously then more luxuriously
testing whether there is anything
worth waking for.

Others at the first faint whiff
of sunshine seem to burst
open with a ping, their leaves
hidden for so long
revealed as fully formed,
rashly declaring that it's Spring.

As sap rises

dare to walk barefoot on the lawn
where recently frost crackled, feel
the grass grow through your toes

low flowers emerge, the celandine
and snowdrop, violet, daisy, wood
anemone, just clearing the ground

frothy dogwood sucking up the dew,
gorse gazing at an avenue of trees
whose younger branches are kissing overhead.

Feminist flower

Kneeling beside the modest snowdrop
try describing it as *brazen hussy*:
you'll find it doesn't work.

At a stretch you might just get away
with using an adjective like that
when speaking of the daffodil;

and yet most of the family narcissus
wait nervously for spring before
they dare to brave the cold and wind,

while the snowdrop has the guts to push
its head through January's iron-clad earth
and even the odd residual patch of snow

flaunting the beauty we describe as delicate,
uncompromising in its declaration
that winter has been overcome.

Candlemas

the flame surges, gutters,
wiggles like a geisha,
stutters then rises to illuminate
your features

as the candle plays
your brightened face
displays emotions
normally well hidden

the shade
as well as the light
of your face is displayed
presented in this sacred place

once again
the flame rises
like a tiny sword
piercing the darkness

Oversteps Books Ltd

Oversteps has previously published books by the following poets: David Grubb, Giles Goodland, Alex Smith, Will Daunt, Patricia Bishop, Christopher Cook, Jan Farquarson, Charles Hadfield, Mandy Pannett, Doris Hulme, James Cole, Helen Kitson, Bill Headdon, Avril Bruton, Ross Cogan, Ann Kelley, Marianne Larsen, Anne Lewis-Smith, Mary Maher, Susan Taylor, Simon Williams, Genista Lewes, Alwyn Marriage, Miriam Darlington, Anne Born, Glen Phillips, A C Clarke, Rebecca Gethin, W H Petty, Melanie Penycate, Andrew Nightingale, Caroline Carver, John Stuart, Ann Segrave, Rose Cook, Jenny Hope, Christopher North, Hilary Elfick, Jennie Osborne, Elisabeth Rowe, Anne Stewart, Oz Hardwick, Angela Stoner, Terry Gifford, Michael Swan, Denise Bennett, Maggie Butt, Anthony Watts, Joan McGavin, Robert Stein, Graham High, Diane Tang and R V Bailey.

Alwyn Marriage's collection, *Touching Earth*, was published by Oversteps Books in 2007.

For details of all these books, information about Oversteps and up-to-date news, please look at our website:
www.overstepsbooks.com